A COLLECTION OF
MY FAVORITE RECIPES

We create our books with love and great care.

Yet mistakes can always happen. For any issues with your recipe book, such as faulty binding, printing errors, or something else, please do not hesitate to contact us at: **hello@happybookshub.com**.
We will make sure you get a replacement copy immediately.

TABLE OF CONTENTS

/PAGE/ /RECIPE NAME/ /NOTES/

TABLE OF CONTENTS

/PAGE/ /RECIPE NAME/ /NOTES/

TABLE OF CONTENTS

/PAGE/ /RECIPE NAME/ /NOTES/

TABLE OF CONTENTS

TABLE OF CONTENTS

INGREDIENTS

....

....

....

....

....

....

DIRECTIONS

....

....

....

....

....

....

....

....

....

....

....

....

RATING

☆ ☆ ☆ ☆ ☆

DIFFICULTY

○ ○ ○ ○ ○

SERVES

1   2   3   4   ...

COOKING TIME

BEST SERVED WITH

....

....

NOTES

....

....

....

....

....

....

....

INGREDIENTS

RATING

☆ ☆ ☆ ☆ ☆

DIFFICULTY

○ ○ ○ ○ ○

SERVES

1   2   3   4   ...

COOKING TIME

DIRECTIONS

BEST SERVED WITH

NOTES

RATING

☆ ☆ ☆ ☆ ☆

INGREDIENTS

DIFFICULTY

○ ○ ○ ○ ○

SERVES

1   2   3   4   ...

COOKING TIME

DIRECTIONS

BEST SERVED WITH

NOTES

INGREDIENTS

DIRECTIONS

RATING

DIFFICULTY

SERVES
1   2   3   4   ...

COOKING TIME

BEST SERVED WITH

NOTES

INGREDIENTS

DIFFICULTY

SERVES

1   2   3   4   ...

COOKING TIME

DIRECTIONS

BEST SERVED WITH

NOTES

INGREDIENTS

DIRECTIONS

RATING

DIFFICULTY

SERVES

1   2   3   4   ...

COOKING TIME

BEST SERVED WITH

NOTES

INGREDIENTS

DIFFICULTY
○ ○ ○ ○ ○

SERVES
1   2   3   4   ...

COOKING TIME

DIRECTIONS

BEST SERVED WITH

NOTES

INGREDIENTS

RATING

DIFFICULTY

○ ○ ○ ○ ○

SERVES

1   2   3   4   ...

COOKING TIME

DIRECTIONS

BEST SERVED WITH

NOTES

INGREDIENTS

RATING

⭐ ⭐ ⭐ ⭐ ⭐

DIFFICULTY

○ ○ ○ ○ ○

SERVES

1　2　3　4　...

COOKING TIME

DIRECTIONS

BEST SERVED WITH

NOTES

INGREDIENTS

RATING

☆ ☆ ☆ ☆ ☆

DIFFICULTY

○ ○ ○ ○ ○

SERVES

1　2　3　4　...

COOKING TIME

DIRECTIONS

BEST SERVED WITH

NOTES

RATING

☆ ☆ ☆ ☆ ☆

INGREDIENTS

DIFFICULTY

○ ○ ○ ○ ○

SERVES

1   2   3   4   ...

COOKING TIME

DIRECTIONS

BEST SERVED WITH

NOTES

INGREDIENTS

RATING

DIFFICULTY

SERVES

1 2 3 4 ...

COOKING TIME

DIRECTIONS

BEST SERVED WITH

NOTES

INGREDIENTS

RATING

DIFFICULTY

○ ○ ○ ○ ○

SERVES

1   2   3   4   ...

COOKING TIME

DIRECTIONS

BEST SERVED WITH

NOTES

14

INGREDIENTS

RATING

☆ ☆ ☆ ☆ ☆

DIFFICULTY

○ ○ ○ ○ ○

SERVES

1   2   3   4   ...

COOKING TIME

DIRECTIONS

BEST SERVED WITH

NOTES

RATING

INGREDIENTS

DIFFICULTY

○ ○ ○ ○ ○

SERVES

1   2   3   4   ...

COOKING TIME

DIRECTIONS

BEST SERVED WITH

NOTES

INGREDIENTS

RATING

DIFFICULTY

SERVES

1　2　3　4　...

COOKING TIME

DIRECTIONS

BEST SERVED WITH

NOTES

17

RATING

☆ ☆ ☆ ☆ ☆

DIFFICULTY

○ ○ ○ ○ ○

INGREDIENTS

SERVES

1   2   3   4   ...

COOKING TIME

DIRECTIONS

BEST SERVED WITH

NOTES

INGREDIENTS

DIRECTIONS

RATING

DIFFICULTY

SERVES

1   2   3   4   ...

COOKING TIME

BEST SERVED WITH

NOTES

_____

INGREDIENTS

RATING

☆ ☆ ☆ ☆ ☆

DIFFICULTY

○ ○ ○ ○ ○

SERVES

1   2   3   4   ...

COOKING TIME

_____

BEST SERVED WITH

DIRECTIONS

NOTES

RATING

☆☆☆☆☆

INGREDIENTS

DIFFICULTY

○ ○ ○ ○ ○

SERVES

1   2   3   4   ...

COOKING TIME

DIRECTIONS

BEST SERVED WITH

NOTES

INGREDIENTS

RATING

DIFFICULTY

○ ○ ○ ○ ○

SERVES

1   2   3   4   ...

COOKING TIME

DIRECTIONS

BEST SERVED WITH

NOTES

22

INGREDIENTS

RATING

DIFFICULTY

○ ○ ○ ○ ○

SERVES

1   2   3   4   ...

COOKING TIME

DIRECTIONS

BEST SERVED WITH

NOTES

INGREDIENTS

RATING

DIFFICULTY

○ ○ ○ ○ ○

SERVES

1   2   3   4   ...

COOKING TIME

DIRECTIONS

BEST SERVED WITH

NOTES

RATING

INGREDIENTS

DIFFICULTY
○ ○ ○ ○ ○

SERVES
1 2 3 4 ...

COOKING TIME

DIRECTIONS

BEST SERVED WITH

NOTES

INGREDIENTS

RATING

DIFFICULTY
○ ○ ○ ○ ○

SERVES
1   2   3   4   ...

COOKING TIME

DIRECTIONS

BEST SERVED WITH

NOTES

INGREDIENTS

RATING

☆ ☆ ☆ ☆ ☆

DIFFICULTY

○ ○ ○ ○ ○

SERVES

1   2   3   4   ...

COOKING TIME

DIRECTIONS

BEST SERVED WITH

NOTES

27

INGREDIENTS

RATING

DIFFICULTY

○ ○ ○ ○ ○

SERVES

1   2   3   4   ...

COOKING TIME

DIRECTIONS

BEST SERVED WITH

NOTES

INGREDIENTS

RATING
☆ ☆ ☆ ☆ ☆

DIFFICULTY
○ ○ ○ ○ ○

SERVES
1   2   3   4   ...

COOKING TIME

DIRECTIONS

BEST SERVED WITH

NOTES

29

INGREDIENTS

RATING

☆ ☆ ☆ ☆ ☆

DIFFICULTY

○ ○ ○ ○ ○

SERVES

1   2   3   4   ...

COOKING TIME

DIRECTIONS

BEST SERVED WITH

NOTES

INGREDIENTS

RATING

DIFFICULTY

SERVES

1   2   3   4   ...

COOKING TIME

DIRECTIONS

BEST SERVED WITH

NOTES

INGREDIENTS

RATING

☆ ☆ ☆ ☆ ☆

DIFFICULTY

○ ○ ○ ○ ○

SERVES

1   2   3   4   ...

COOKING TIME

DIRECTIONS

BEST SERVED WITH

NOTES

INGREDIENTS

RATING

☆☆☆☆☆

DIFFICULTY

○ ○ ○ ○ ○

SERVES

1   2   3   4   ...

COOKING TIME

DIRECTIONS

BEST SERVED WITH

NOTES

INGREDIENTS

RATING

DIFFICULTY

SERVES

1   2   3   4   ...

COOKING TIME

DIRECTIONS

BEST SERVED WITH

NOTES

34

INGREDIENTS

DIRECTIONS

RATING

☆ ☆ ☆ ☆ ☆

DIFFICULTY

○ ○ ○ ○ ○

SERVES

1   2   3   4   ...

COOKING TIME

BEST SERVED WITH

NOTES

INGREDIENTS

RATING

DIFFICULTY

○ ○ ○ ○ ○

SERVES

1   2   3   4   ...

🕐

COOKING TIME

DIRECTIONS

BEST SERVED WITH

✎

NOTES

36

INGREDIENTS

DIRECTIONS

RATING
☆ ☆ ☆ ☆ ☆

DIFFICULTY
○ ○ ○ ○ ○

SERVES
1   2   3   4   ...

COOKING TIME

BEST SERVED WITH

NOTES

37

INGREDIENTS

RATING

☆ ☆ ☆ ☆ ☆

DIFFICULTY

○ ○ ○ ○ ○

SERVES

1   2   3   4   ...

COOKING TIME

DIRECTIONS

BEST SERVED WITH

NOTES

INGREDIENTS

DIRECTIONS

RATING

☆☆☆☆☆

DIFFICULTY

○ ○ ○ ○ ○

SERVES

1   2   3   4   ...

COOKING TIME

BEST SERVED WITH

NOTES

39

INGREDIENTS

RATING

DIFFICULTY

○ ○ ○ ○ ○

SERVES

1   2   3   4   ...

COOKING TIME

DIRECTIONS

BEST SERVED WITH

NOTES

INGREDIENTS

RATING

DIFFICULTY

○ ○ ○ ○ ○

SERVES

1   2   3   4   ...

COOKING TIME

DIRECTIONS

BEST SERVED WITH

NOTES

41

INGREDIENTS

RATING

☆ ☆ ☆ ☆ ☆

DIFFICULTY

○ ○ ○ ○ ○

SERVES

1   2   3   4   ...

COOKING TIME

DIRECTIONS

BEST SERVED WITH

NOTES

INGREDIENTS

RATING

DIFFICULTY

SERVES

1   2   3   4   ...

COOKING TIME

DIRECTIONS

BEST SERVED WITH

NOTES

43

INGREDIENTS

DIRECTIONS

RATING

DIFFICULTY
○ ○ ○ ○ ○

SERVES
1   2   3   4   ...

COOKING TIME

BEST SERVED WITH

NOTES

INGREDIENTS

DIRECTIONS

45

INGREDIENTS

RATING

☆ ☆ ☆ ☆ ☆

DIFFICULTY

○ ○ ○ ○ ○

SERVES

1   2   3   4   ...

COOKING TIME

DIRECTIONS

BEST SERVED WITH

NOTES

46

INGREDIENTS

RATING

DIFFICULTY

SERVES

1   2   3   4   ...

COOKING TIME

DIRECTIONS

BEST SERVED WITH

NOTES

47

INGREDIENTS

RATING

DIFFICULTY

SERVES

1　2　3　4　...

COOKING TIME

DIRECTIONS

BEST SERVED WITH

NOTES

48

INGREDIENTS

DIRECTIONS

RATING

☆ ☆ ☆ ☆ ☆

DIFFICULTY

○ ○ ○ ○ ○

SERVES

1   2   3   4   ...

COOKING TIME

BEST SERVED WITH

NOTES

49

INGREDIENTS

RATING

☆ ☆ ☆ ☆ ☆

DIFFICULTY

○ ○ ○ ○ ○

SERVES

1   2   3   4   ...

COOKING TIME

DIRECTIONS

BEST SERVED WITH

NOTES

RATING

☆ ☆ ☆ ☆ ☆

INGREDIENTS

DIFFICULTY

○ ○ ○ ○ ○

SERVES

1   2   3   4   ...

COOKING TIME

DIRECTIONS

BEST SERVED WITH

NOTES

51

INGREDIENTS

RATING
☆ ☆ ☆ ☆ ☆

DIFFICULTY
○ ○ ○ ○ ○

SERVES
1   2   3   4   ...

COOKING TIME

DIRECTIONS

BEST SERVED WITH

NOTES

52

INGREDIENTS

RATING

DIFFICULTY
○ ○ ○ ○ ○

SERVES
1   2   3   4   ...

COOKING TIME

DIRECTIONS

BEST SERVED WITH

NOTES

53

INGREDIENTS

RATING

☆ ☆ ☆ ☆ ☆

DIFFICULTY

○ ○ ○ ○ ○

SERVES

1   2   3   4   ...

COOKING TIME

DIRECTIONS

BEST SERVED WITH

NOTES

INGREDIENTS

RATING

☆☆☆☆☆

DIFFICULTY

○ ○ ○ ○ ○

SERVES

1 2 3 4 ...

COOKING TIME

DIRECTIONS

BEST SERVED WITH

NOTES

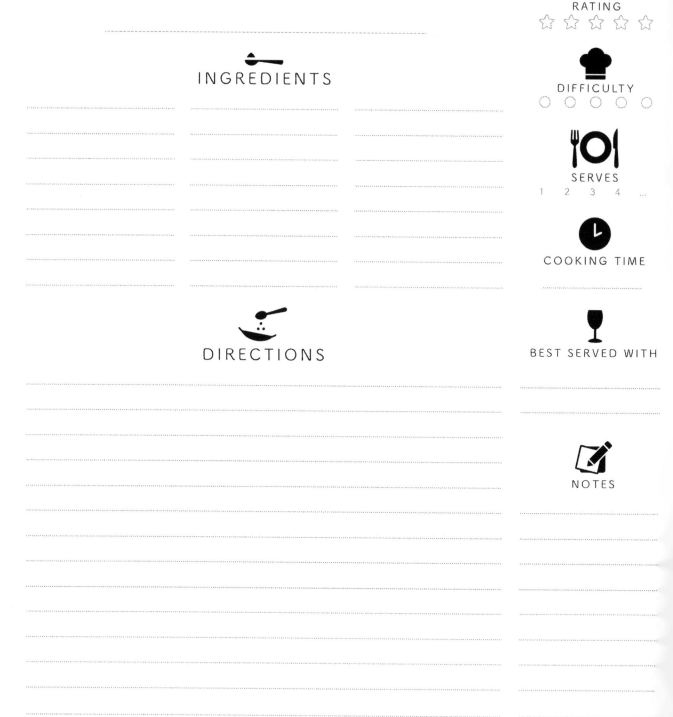

55

INGREDIENTS

_____
_____
_____
_____
_____
_____
_____

DIRECTIONS

_____
_____
_____
_____
_____
_____
_____
_____
_____
_____
_____
_____

RATING
☆ ☆ ☆ ☆ ☆

DIFFICULTY
○ ○ ○ ○ ○

SERVES
1   2   3   4   ...

COOKING TIME
_____

BEST SERVED WITH
_____
_____

NOTES
_____
_____
_____
_____
_____

56

RATING

☆ ☆ ☆ ☆ ☆

INGREDIENTS

DIFFICULTY

○ ○ ○ ○ ○

🍴◯🔪

SERVES

1   2   3   4   ...

🕐

COOKING TIME

DIRECTIONS

🍷

BEST SERVED WITH

📝

NOTES

57

INGREDIENTS

RATING

☆ ☆ ☆ ☆ ☆

DIFFICULTY

○ ○ ○ ○ ○

SERVES

1   2   3   4   ...

🕐

COOKING TIME

DIRECTIONS

🍷

BEST SERVED WITH

📝

NOTES

58

INGREDIENTS

RATING

DIFFICULTY

SERVES
1   2   3   4   ...

COOKING TIME

DIRECTIONS

BEST SERVED WITH

NOTES

INGREDIENTS

DIRECTIONS

RATING

DIFFICULTY
○ ○ ○ ○ ○

SERVES
1   2   3   4   ...

COOKING TIME

BEST SERVED WITH

NOTES

INGREDIENTS

RATING

DIFFICULTY

SERVES

1   2   3   4   ...

COOKING TIME

DIRECTIONS

BEST SERVED WITH

NOTES

61

INGREDIENTS

RATING

DIFFICULTY

○ ○ ○ ○ ○

SERVES

1   2   3   4   ...

COOKING TIME

DIRECTIONS

BEST SERVED WITH

NOTES

62

INGREDIENTS

RATING

☆ ☆ ☆ ☆ ☆

DIFFICULTY

○ ○ ○ ○ ○

SERVES

1   2   3   4   ...

COOKING TIME

DIRECTIONS

BEST SERVED WITH

NOTES

63

INGREDIENTS

DIRECTIONS

RATING
☆ ☆ ☆ ☆ ☆

DIFFICULTY
○ ○ ○ ○ ○

SERVES
1   2   3   4   ...

COOKING TIME

BEST SERVED WITH

NOTES

INGREDIENTS

RATING

DIFFICULTY

SERVES

1   2   3   4   ...

COOKING TIME

DIRECTIONS

BEST SERVED WITH

NOTES

INGREDIENTS

RATING

DIFFICULTY

○ ○ ○ ○ ○

SERVES

1   2   3   4   ...

COOKING TIME

DIRECTIONS

BEST SERVED WITH

NOTES

66

INGREDIENTS

DIRECTIONS

RATING
☆ ☆ ☆ ☆ ☆

DIFFICULTY
○ ○ ○ ○ ○

SERVES
1   2   3   4   ...

COOKING TIME

BEST SERVED WITH

NOTES

67

INGREDIENTS

RATING

DIFFICULTY

○ ○ ○ ○ ○

🍴🍽️🔪

SERVES

1   2   3   4   ...

🕐

COOKING TIME

DIRECTIONS

🍷

BEST SERVED WITH

NOTES

68

INGREDIENTS

RATING

☆ ☆ ☆ ☆ ☆

DIFFICULTY

○ ○ ○ ○ ○

SERVES

1   2   3   4   ...

COOKING TIME

DIRECTIONS

BEST SERVED WITH

NOTES

INGREDIENTS

RATING

DIFFICULTY

SERVES
1   2   3   4   ...

COOKING TIME

DIRECTIONS

BEST SERVED WITH

NOTES

70

INGREDIENTS

RATING

☆☆☆☆☆

DIFFICULTY

○ ○ ○ ○ ○

SERVES

1   2   3   4   ...

COOKING TIME

DIRECTIONS

BEST SERVED WITH

NOTES

71

INGREDIENTS

DIRECTIONS

RATING

DIFFICULTY

○ ○ ○ ○ ○

SERVES

1   2   3   4   ...

COOKING TIME

BEST SERVED WITH

NOTES

INGREDIENTS

RATING

DIFFICULTY

○ ○ ○ ○ ○

SERVES

1 2 3 4 ...

🕐

COOKING TIME

DIRECTIONS

🍷

BEST SERVED WITH

📝

NOTES

73

RATING
☆ ☆ ☆ ☆ ☆

INGREDIENTS

DIFFICULTY
○ ○ ○ ○ ○

SERVES
1   2   3   4   ...

COOKING TIME

DIRECTIONS

BEST SERVED WITH

NOTES

INGREDIENTS

RATING

☆ ☆ ☆ ☆ ☆

DIFFICULTY

○ ○ ○ ○ ○

SERVES

1   2   3   4   ...

COOKING TIME

DIRECTIONS

BEST SERVED WITH

NOTES

RATING

☆ ☆ ☆ ☆ ☆

INGREDIENTS

DIFFICULTY

○ ○ ○ ○ ○

SERVES

1   2   3   4   ...

COOKING TIME

DIRECTIONS

BEST SERVED WITH

NOTES

INGREDIENTS

RATING

DIFFICULTY

SERVES

1   2   3   4   ...

COOKING TIME

DIRECTIONS

BEST SERVED WITH

NOTES

77

INGREDIENTS

RATING

DIFFICULTY

○ ○ ○ ○ ○

SERVES

1　2　3　4　...

COOKING TIME

DIRECTIONS

BEST SERVED WITH

NOTES

INGREDIENTS

RATING

☆☆☆☆☆

DIFFICULTY

○ ○ ○ ○ ○

SERVES

1   2   3   4   ...

COOKING TIME

DIRECTIONS

BEST SERVED WITH

NOTES

INGREDIENTS

RATING

DIFFICULTY

SERVES
1 2 3 4 ...

COOKING TIME

DIRECTIONS

BEST SERVED WITH

NOTES

INGREDIENTS

RATING

☆ ☆ ☆ ☆ ☆

DIFFICULTY

○ ○ ○ ○ ○

SERVES

1   2   3   4   ...

COOKING TIME

DIRECTIONS

BEST SERVED WITH

NOTES

81

INGREDIENTS

RATING
☆ ☆ ☆ ☆ ☆

DIFFICULTY
○ ○ ○ ○ ○

SERVES
1   2   3   4   ...

COOKING TIME

DIRECTIONS

BEST SERVED WITH

NOTES

INGREDIENTS

DIRECTIONS

RATING

DIFFICULTY

SERVES

1   2   3   4   ...

COOKING TIME

BEST SERVED WITH

NOTES

83

INGREDIENTS

DIFFICULTY

SERVES
1 2 3 4 ...

COOKING TIME

DIRECTIONS

BEST SERVED WITH

NOTES

RATING

☆ ☆ ☆ ☆

INGREDIENTS

DIFFICULTY
○ ○ ○ ○ ○

SERVES
1   2   3   4   ...

COOKING TIME

DIRECTIONS

BEST SERVED WITH

NOTES

85

RATING

☆ ☆ ☆ ☆ ☆

INGREDIENTS

DIFFICULTY

○ ○ ○ ○ ○

SERVES

1   2   3   4   ...

COOKING TIME

DIRECTIONS

BEST SERVED WITH

NOTES

86

INGREDIENTS

RATING
☆ ☆ ☆ ☆ ☆

DIFFICULTY
○ ○ ○ ○ ○

SERVES
1   2   3   4   ...

COOKING TIME

DIRECTIONS

BEST SERVED WITH

NOTES

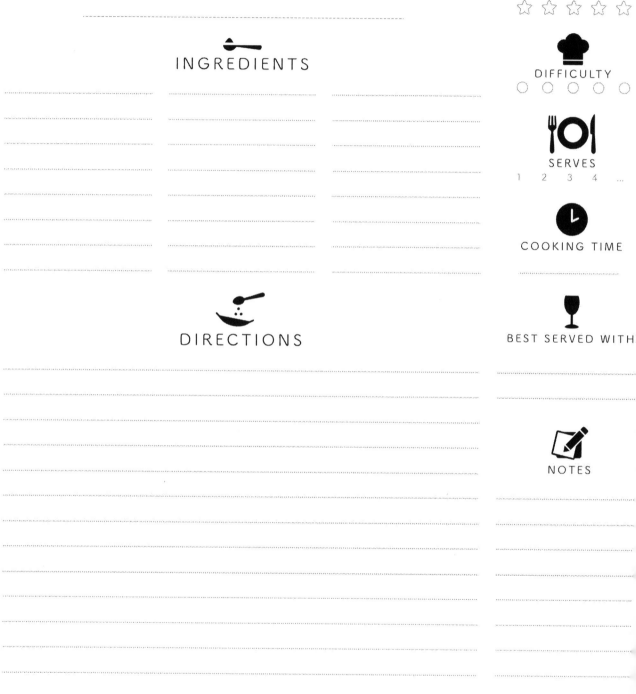

INGREDIENTS

RATING

DIFFICULTY

SERVES

1 2 3 4 ...

COOKING TIME

DIRECTIONS

BEST SERVED WITH

NOTES

INGREDIENTS

....

....

....

....

....

....

....

DIRECTIONS

....

....

....

....

....

....

....

....

....

....

....

....

....

RATING

☆ ☆ ☆ ☆ ☆

DIFFICULTY

○ ○ ○ ○ ○

SERVES

1   2   3   4   ...

COOKING TIME

....

BEST SERVED WITH

....

....

NOTES

....

....

....

....

....

....

....

....

....

RATING

INGREDIENTS

DIFFICULTY

○ ○ ○ ○ ○

SERVES

1 2 3 4 ...

COOKING TIME

DIRECTIONS

BEST SERVED WITH

NOTES

90

RATING

INGREDIENTS

DIFFICULTY

○ ○ ○ ○ ○

SERVES

1   2   3   4   ...

COOKING TIME

DIRECTIONS

BEST SERVED WITH

NOTES

91

INGREDIENTS

DIFFICULTY
○ ○ ○ ○ ○

SERVES
1   2   3   4   ...

COOKING TIME

DIRECTIONS

BEST SERVED WITH

NOTES

92

INGREDIENTS

RATING

☆ ☆ ☆ ☆ ☆

DIFFICULTY

○ ○ ○ ○ ○

SERVES

1   2   3   4   ...

COOKING TIME

DIRECTIONS

BEST SERVED WITH

NOTES

93

INGREDIENTS

RATING

☆☆☆☆☆

DIFFICULTY

○ ○ ○ ○ ○

SERVES

1   2   3   4   ...

COOKING TIME

DIRECTIONS

BEST SERVED WITH

NOTES

94

INGREDIENTS

RATING

DIFFICULTY

SERVES

1   2   3   4   ...

COOKING TIME

DIRECTIONS

BEST SERVED WITH

NOTES

95

INGREDIENTS

RATING

☆ ☆ ☆ ☆ ☆

DIFFICULTY

○ ○ ○ ○ ○

SERVES

1   2   3   4

COOKING TIME

DIRECTIONS

BEST SERVED WITH

NOTES

96

INGREDIENTS

DIRECTIONS

RATING

☆ ☆ ☆ ☆ ☆

DIFFICULTY

○ ○ ○ ○ ○

SERVES

1   2   3   4   ...

COOKING TIME

BEST SERVED WIT

NOTES

97

INGREDIENTS

DIRECTIONS

RATING

☆ ☆ ☆ ☆ ☆

DIFFICULTY

○ ○ ○ ○ ○

SERVES

1   2   3   4   ...

COOKING TIME

BEST SERVED WITH

NOTES

INGREDIENTS

DIRECTIONS

RATING

☆ ☆ ☆ ☆ ☆

DIFFICULTY

○ ○ ○ ○ ○

SERVES

1   2   3   4   ...

COOKING TIME

BEST SERVED WIT

NOTES

INGREDIENTS

RATING

☆ ☆ ☆ ☆ ☆

DIFFICULTY

○ ○ ○ ○ ○

SERVES

1   2   3   4   ...

COOKING TIME

DIRECTIONS

BEST SERVED WITH

NOTES

INGREDIENTS

DIRECTIONS

RATING

☆ ☆ ☆ ☆ ☆

DIFFICULTY

○ ○ ○ ○ ○

SERVES

1   2   3   4   ...

COOKING TIME

BEST SERVED WITH

NOTES

HANDY KITCHEN REFERENCES

CUPS, SPOONS & LIQUIDS

Measure	Ounces	Equivalents	Metric
1/4 tsp			1 ml
1/2 tsp			2.5 ml
1 tsp		1/3 Tbsp	5 ml
2 tsp	1/3 fl oz	2/3 Tbsp	10 ml
1 Tbsp	1/2 fl oz	3 tsp	15 ml (15 cc)
2 Tbsp	1 fl oz	1/8 cup (6 tsp)	30 ml (30 cc)
1/4 cup	2 fl oz	4 Tbsp	60 ml
1/3 cup	2 2/3 fl oz	5 Tbsp & 1 tsp	80 ml
1/2 cup	4 fl oz	8 Tbsp	120 ml
2/3 cup	5 1/3 fl oz	10 Tbsp & 2 tsp	160 ml
3/4 cup	6 fl oz	12 Tbsp	180 ml
7/8 cup	7 fl oz	14 Tbsp	200 ml
1 cup (1/2 pint)	8 fl oz	16 Tbsp	250 ml
2 cups (1 pint)	16 fl oz	32 Tbsp	500 ml
1 quart	32 fl oz	4 cups	950 ml
1 quart plus 1/4 cup	34 fl oz	4 cups & 4 Tbsp	1 liter (1000ml)
1 gallon (4 quarts)	128 fl oz	16 cups	3.8 liters

WEIGHT

Ounces	Pounds	Grams
1/4 ounce		7 grams
1/2 ounce		15 grams
3/4 ounce		21 grams
1 ounce		28 grams
2 ounces		57 grams
3 ounces		85 grams
4 ounces	1/4 pound	113 grams
8 ounces	1/2 pound	227 grams
16 ounces	1 pound	454 grams
35.2 ounces	2.2 pounds	1 kilogram

TEMPERATURE

Fahrenheit	Celsius	Old School
250° F	120° C	Very cool oven
275° F	140° C	Cool oven
300° F	150° C	Cool oven
325° F	160° C	Very moderate oven
350° F	180° C	Moderate oven
375° F	190° C	Moderate oven
400° F	200° C	Moderately hot oven
425° F	220° C	Hot oven
450° F	230° C	Hot oven
475° F	245° C	Very hot oven

COMMON INGREDIENT WEIGHTS

Ingredient	Volume	Weight (ounces)	Weight (grams)
all purpose flour	1 cup	4.5 oz	125 g
	1 Tbsp	0.3 oz	8 g
	1 tsp		3 g
bread flour	1 cup	4.5 oz	125 g
whole wheat flour	1 cup	4.5 oz	125 g
water	1 cup	8.3 oz	235 g
butter	1 cup	8 oz	230 g
milk	1 cup	8.5 oz	240 g
oil	1 cup	7.5 oz	210 g
heavy cream	1 cup	8 oz	230 g
sour cream	1 cup	8.5 oz	240 g
yogurt	1 cup	8.5 oz	240 g
white granulated sugar	1 cup	7 oz	200 g
	1 Tbsp	0.5 oz	14 g
	1 tsp		4 g
brown sugar	1 cup	7.5 oz	210 g
powdered sugar	1 cup	4 oz	115 g
honey	1 cup	11.75 oz	335 g
corn syrup	1 cup	11.5 oz	330 g
salt	1 Tbsp		15 g
	1 tsp		7 g
1 large egg (in the shell)		2 oz	55 g
1 large egg (without shell)		1.75 oz	50 g
baking powder	1 tsp		5 g
baking soda	1 tsp		5 g
yeast, instant	1 tsp		3 g
yeast, active dry	1 tsp		3 g
cocoa	1 cup	3.25 oz	90 g
raisins	1 cup	5 oz	145 g
chopped nuts	1 cup	6.7 oz	190 g

HEY THERE!

This blank recipe journal is brought to you by Happy Books Hub. We have a passion for creating books that can improve and add joy to people's lives. Hopefully this book will accomplish just that for you!

If you have any suggestions on how to improve it, or what we can change or add to make it more useful particularly to you, please don't hesitate to contact us at **happybookshub@gmail.com** We would be more than happy to consider how to apply your suggestion to this journal's next edition.

Thank you for buying My Favorite Recipes journal!

Please, support us and leave a review!

Love,
Happy Books Hub

Other books by Happy Books Hub you might enjoy:

Hello New Me:
A Daily Food and Exercise Journal to Help You Become the Best Version of Yourself

Start With Gratitude:
A Daily Gratitude Journal | Positivity Diary for a Happier You in Just 5 Minutes a Day

My 66-Day Challenge Habit Tracker & Goal Planner:
A Daily Journal to Help You Track Your Habits and Achieve Your Dream Life

Love,
Happy Books Hub

Made in the USA
Middletown, DE
11 December 2020